THE TWO OF US

Lloyd Rees

Published by
Llyfrau Cambria Books, Wales, United Kingdom.
*Cambria Books is a division of
Cambria Publishing Ltd.*
Discover our other books at: www.cambriabooks.co.uk

Lloyd Rees

Lloyd Rees was born in London in 1949. He grew up in Swansea and was educated in Swansea and Sussex. He began writing poetry in the late nineteen eighties but it was his fiction that was published first. His debut novel was shortlisted for BBC Wales Book of the Year in 1993. His poetry has appeared in a number of magazines and anthologies and he was shortlisted for a Bridport Poetry Prize in 2000. This book is his fifth volume of poems.

Also by Lloyd Rees

Poetry

To Liu and All Mankind (with Alan Perry)

Mangoes on the Moon

Swansea Poems

Simple Arithmetic

Fiction

Don't Stand So Close

The Show-Me State

Voices Without Parts

For Rachel

and Ainsley

and in memory of Olive (1913-1986)

CONTENTS

MOTHER AND SON

FATHER AND DAUGHTER

MAN AND WOMAN

MAN

MOTHER AND SON

RELEASE DATE

I called her 'The Mother' as if it were a title,
but 'Ma' to her face because it sounded harder
than mam or mummy – she was too brittle
and she came and went more like a warder.

I only muttered the odd word, as little
enough, in truth, as I could afford her,
and then beneath the scream of the old kettle.
Anyway, I was only a type of boarder.

Till one day, eighteen, clutching a UCAS letter,
I touched her arm. 'I'm in,' I said, 'I'm off.'
She looked sick-delighted; I'd caught her
off duty apparently. She gave a sort of cough
and said, 'That's good, son.' She wasn't bitter,
nor, as I later saw, anything like tough.

A GAMBLE

She's been a gambler in her day:
a hundred quid on a horse one time;
the buzz must have been immense,
the loss unbelievable-sublime.

She taught me card games, made me stay
up late and play for coins or straws.
She could do the two thumb shuffle;
I felt I was breaking all the laws.

Her one big gamble didn't pay:
she quit her small town roots and sailed
to London. Worked in shops and pubs,
tried everything she could and failed.

Back in her dirty little town she bought
on tick the spuds, the eggs, the bread;
forgot about the flaunted wealth
and shuffled part-time cleaning jobs instead.

THE WRECK

I called her The Kipper – a simple pun –
because she always seemed to be asleep.
I watched her drowning in her meagre life,
disappearing into some impassive deep.

Sharp poverty had whittled her to bone
and dazed her eyes and slacked her jaw.
She rotted in the doldrums of her days
as if there'd never been a life before.

She'd slump there in her chair – moquette –
as if discarded by some other.
She was a too deep valiant wreck
even before I knew she was my mother.

Some storms come silently, it seems,
and crack the sides of thoughts and dreams.

SOUNDTRACK

She sang about the 'pyramids along the Nile'
as, in her belted coat and premature stoop,
she dragged me down some windy street
to buy some rubbish from the Walkaround Shop.

Or, in our lean-to kitchen, she'd attempt
a whistled 'Apple Blossom Time'
while I bounced a ball against a wall
and listened for anything that would rhyme.

She liked 'Your Hundred Best Tunes' - a mélange
of arias and racy bits from symphonies.
I despaired of ever growing up and away;
I longed for my own record player and LPs.

I don't listen to music much these days.
I don't even whistle as I trudge from shop
to dreary shop. I wear a coat myself,
but I will not, will not stoop.

THE OLD HOUSE

Light, paper-thin and blank
lies down in the old room.
There are china ornaments to mime
some false bucolic past
but all that's really here is dust
and the wreck of a life sunk.

And this space seems smaller now;
the yellowing ceiling lower;
the years have shrunk even air
and the house's worn ribs are tight
with the tightness of a hospital sheet.
Here a life went stale and slow.

The veneered door to the kitchenette
is open – linoleum and tiles
and empty cupboards, smells
of ancient parazone and lard.
Here the old ghosts remain unheard;
her life was a pointless habit.

And yet, in this living room
there's an ugly old upright
where she used to take her seat
and hammer out a slow waltz
that clunked against the papered walls
of her simply furnished tomb.

She learned to play too late;
her fingers struggled to reach
the keys that were meant to catch
the melodies she heard inside.
I try to close that grim lid
but I still hear her waltzing heart.

DIFFERENT TASTES

When I was eight – eight!
my mother made me read a book.
'Enough of those comics,' she suddenly said.
'They'll rot your mind. But this is good. Look.'

I couldn't believe how big it was,
a brown vellum *Dombey and Son*.
and how small the print.
I couldn't believe there was no more fun.

I waded through endless sentences.
It was like running uphill through sand.
Life went dark. Square-jawed Tommies smashing the Hun
gave way to nuances I couldn't understand.

It was about a pale young boy too frail
for the hearty world, I think it meant.
Something like that. Or it may have been
about something completely different.

She wanted me to know of finer things
than had come her way.
She made me listen to Bach,
took me to numb my mind at ballet.

I wanted jokes and adventures,
Blitzkrieg, schnell, achtung, kerpow.
I've changed. I want softer days.
I'd appreciate those nuances now.

LONE PARENTING

'You haven't got a father!' The rage
was shocking. She was always quietly spoken.
But I knew I must have one. Somewhere.

I'd reached a certain questioning age
where trust can be broken
and I thought it just wasn't fair.

'I saw my birth certificate,' I said.
'His name was on it. So I know.'
Her face slumped, fell apart.

'You'll never see him now. He's dead.
It all happened a long time ago.'
I wondered about her small heart.

'So never ask again. Don't. Please.'
I had to obey. At least for now.
We turned to other things.

Now I'm the age she was
back then. I have to know
and heed what each day brings.

BURDEN

We'd decided on a day at the beach,

the sun a harsh white gold,

but the soft tide a stroll away.

I'd insisted my mother come along,

though the walk down through the woods

was far too long and exhausting.

I wanted to repay the days at the Slip

where I'd sat in the dullness

shivering in a bather,

half-listening to her stories.

She didn't have a costume,

but she had some safety pins

in her bag.

She pinned together

her vest and her underwear.

I looked away.

Then she began to whimper.
She wanted to go home but
she couldn't face the trek
back up the huge dunes.

I was thirty five, she was twice my age.
I picked her up, my own Anchises,
and stumbled up the sand
like a soldier on exercise.
I wanted to get her home.
Above all, I wanted not to be seen
carrying an old woman,
a big foetus in my arms,
as if running from a fire.

I've carried her since too,
a heavy burden.
But not in my arms.

PATTERN

Poverty grained her face like dirt,
soiled her clothes with its misery,
but she would not take the garments
cast aside by others. Instead,
with a soldier's pragmatism,
she made things out of remnants.

I'd slouch back home from school
to see the threadbare floor awash
with flimsy pattern shapes,
tobacco paper thin,
the geometry of making do.
I'd step past carefully.

McCalls and Butterick meant nothing;
I couldn't see the whole like her.
She knew the yoke, the bias,
the collar, how to fold and trim
and hem her scraps of cotton.
She understood the pattern.

THE COAT

For years she wore a bright red coat,
a splash of lipstick brightness
on the grey of everything.

She'd wear it in the house
to save on the electric,
while I would run about the garden.

I touched it once,
it was coarse like a mat
and I hated it.

She must have loved it though.
Years later I saw it in her wardrobe
sheathed in a plastic caul.

It might have been a gift.
How could a seven year old know?
But I don't think it was.

Perhaps she saw herself in a wood
picking bluebells, a song
on her bright full lips.

Or waltzing through her day
at some holiday camp,
to the summer sun's new tunes.

The fabric soft
and luscious,
lovely to the touch.

ARGUMENT

Ma loved to argue things,

and often things she didn't know a thing about.

I'd be eleven, and, like her,

rigid with certainties, untouched by doubt.

She'd claim that plastic was the devil's work,

or that the Liberals were to blame;

I'd started Grammar School,

I knew everything by Latin name.

She'd argue grey was white or black.

I'd offer her a *QED*,

a *quid pro quo*, a *sine qua non*,

and hate the way she looked at me.

And then she stopped. Gave up.

I couldn't rouse her any more

to say that the sun went round the moon

or Italy was to blame for the war.

I tried provoking, cajoling her

into some new ludicrous argument,

but she'd simply smile, defer to me,

which was never, I swear, my real intent.

DINNER FOR TWO

Three or four small boiled potatoes
and scrag end of lamb.
Or a single piece of ham
and two window sill-ripened tomatoes.

Sterilized milk a week or more old.
Hot water on an orange slice.
Sugar on everything, even rice.
Everything screaming hot, or cold.

An egg, though this was seldom enough.
Lard for chips, that glorious treat.
Always always not enough to eat
and so often thin and gruesome stuff.

She'd make each meal as if it was
our last, with thought and care;
a banquet for the two of us to share
singing to herself 'Because…'

I dine on different foods these

days: a bisque, a ragout or a tagine.

she wouldn't know what these even mean,

but I don't sing such soft melodies.

THE VIOLIN

I hated it:

the screech

the rosin

the tightening and slackening of the bow

as if that would

stop the yowl.

I hated going to

that dapper man

who taught me,

nudged my elbow up

and spoke in quavers.

I hated practising,

thought the yellow duster

on my clavicle

was dandy nonsense,

hated being watched

and feeling failure's spreading stain .

I wanted a harmonica,
something pocketable
something straight and hard
that would howl my adolescent agonies
in twelve bar truth.

Instead I had a violin,
all curves and curlicues
to vibrato that the world
was sweet and painless,
to keep my chin and elbow up.

It was my mother's fault.
She wanted to transport
her only son
to some strange land
where Brahms was king
and rosin soothed all ills.

I just wanted to listen
to Radio Luxemburg at night
to block out all those

waltzes and minuets

and find out stuff

I'd need to know

about love

and love's betrayals.

GOING BACK

At thirty, say, or even twenty eight,
I'd go round once a week,
relate the happenings, or what
might pass for them. I'd seek
out anecdotes or funny quotes.
She'd listen, eyes sagged shut,
and murmur that I shouldn't fret,
it would all turn out alright.

The room, much smaller than before,
was dusty dark and cold;
two chairs, a piano and a two bar fire.
'I don't need any more, I'm old,'
she'd say. I'd try to stay an hour,
each minute ticking slower
as the evening drained both me and her,
and another cup of tea would be no cure.

I'd ask about an uncle or an aunt
(she didn't know the people next door).
but there was never news. They weren't
in touch, she'd say, not any more.
I'd go to water her one rubber plant,
'Don't do that.' 'Why not?' 'Just don't.'
she'd say, 'It's not something I want.'
'Okay,' I'd say, 'I won't.'

And then it was time to go.
Somehow the hour would pass.
with all the little we had to say.
An hour exactly, I couldn't do less.
And I would rise reluctantly
and we would say a fond goodbye,
though never hug or say, 'Love you.'
This was our way to try and stay true.

INSTRUCTOR

She decided to learn to drive
when she was sixty odd.
I thought this was mad
and I told her so, but said I'd give
her lessons if she wanted.
She clutched the wheel
and peered, as if through a grille,
at the deadly road ahead.

She revved like mad, scarcely got out of second.
I feared for my car
but she couldn't hear
as I tutted and groaned.
I should have shown more courage;
the road ahead is always
always dangerous
no matter what your age.

CARING

She got to seventy, wheezed
and spluttered into an eighth decade,
and knocked herself into neutral.
'I've got a carer now,' she said.
'She comes in, brings me meals,
sorts things out around the house.'
I listened, having heard the tales
of social services' casual abuse.

'I'll try and call around more often,'
I sighed. I knew I wouldn't though.
I wanted to hear myself soften,
but also I just wanted to go.
'Do these people take care of you?'
'They do their job,' she said.
 I pictured a matron in institutional blue
insisting my mother get back into bed;
a Teutonic woman of middle years
with no nonsense hair and bold blue eyes.

People care for money, it appears,
and I'm surprised at my own surprise.
Ma looked at me. 'You're doing well,'
she said. Nothing further from the truth.
Then she retreated back into her shell
to make me feel her soft reproof.

WORKING CLASS

She moved from job to job.
I scarcely noticed, such is childhood's solecism,
except she seemed to leave the house at different times.
One day she was a barmaid in The Bush,
skinny arms straining against the stubborn pumps;
the next an usherette; back leaning against the weight
of Kia-Oras, Mivvis and choc ices in her interlude tray.
She tried out forecourt attendant, but self-serve arrived;
she polished floors in offices, the buffer too heavy;
she waited on tables in lunchtime cafes ,
plate after plate of corned beef hash;
anything you didn't need training for.

'You have to get an education,' she said,
 'I don't want this for you.'
I turned to my notes, the seven causes
of the American War of Independence,
the sine or tan of something or other,
and wondered about how to escape my class.

THE FLICKS

She loved the movies. They filled my mother's head.
She lived for Technicolor, she once said.
She took me to the Plaza and The Albert Hall
every Monday afternoon, straight after school

Of course, Ma picked which flick and I obeyed
(I wanted a half time Orange Maid)
It wasn't the expensive treat it should have been,
though I remember every film I've seen.

I sat through hours and days of Doris Day
and wished that bright gay world would go away;
I preferred the dark and grainy danger
of men like Tyrone Power and Stewart Grainger.

We'd sit in silence through the matinee,
then emerge from the darkness into the day,
me, still thinking of the Guns of Navarone,
her, imagining Rita Hayworth all alone.

These are my flickering memories,

worn red plush, my choc ice spilled on my knees,

an empty auditorium,

just me and my dreaming faded mum.

FATHER AND DAUGHTER

FEARS

At bristling three she was a termagant,
 a shrew in size and temper. Nonetheless
I loved her for her certainties, her scant
regard for me and all my fatherliness.

But as she grew and doubts began to bite
she sought out explanations for her fears:
I brushed away the monsters, cast a light
upon the shadowed corners, dabbed her tears.

Or thought I did. Though stories ended well,
they were just fictions, parent tricks to please.
I knew inside, though yet I couldn't tell,
I'd never banish all anxieties.

She's fully grown and looks like me, they say.
It's my turn now to fret the nights away.

SAILORS

I always hoped you'd be the same as me;
but better, more omniscient, less in doubt,
although I feared you'd turn inexorably,
reject my so called wisdoms and sail out
to seas and worlds beyond my harboured life.
I wove long tales and painted dreams with you
of how, as sister, one day mother, wife,
you'd do everything you'd ever want to do.

You tell me now I shouldn't have told you lies;
you never had that sailor in your heart.
I know how failure leaps up to surprise;
I see it in my own dejected art.

We are not different at last, it seems;
so much for navigation and for dreams.

LOST

Never so filled with despair
I ran through that concourse
as if I was on fire,
a father filled with a father's force.

She was gone, some savage
had dragged her to a cubicle in the gents,
to be left, left doll-limp and ravaged.
It made no other sense.

You *do* actually tear at your hair;
I could feel the clumps in my palms,
I pleaded with the surly officials there
as I pulled at my own empty arms.

What she look like? they said.
They were bored, didn't care,
She could actually be dead!
What you say she wear?

A dress, a sari, I corrected myself.
Colour? Blue. Light blue. Sapphire.
She's very pretty. And she's only twelve.
She looks almost oriental, has jet black hair.

We were in Changi, Singapore,
the world's largest airport
and every girl suddenly looked like her.
Knowledge is the cruellest part.

An hour flashed by, the sun fell outside.
The concourse is over two miles long
but I ran it twice over, dying inside,
hoping and screaming to be, for once, wrong.

Then they found her, asleep. She'd crawled
underneath a row of red plastic chairs.
I let my heart slow, as I stared, appalled
at what might have come to pass.

I was broken by my own fears.
She smiled benignly. I hope we don't miss
our flight, she said. Then she saw my tears.
There there, she said, and gave me a kiss.

She didn't get raped or die,
as I was always afraid she might.
She woke to her own life and oh I
miss her on her different flight.

THE ARTISTS

One thoughtful day I asked my painter friend
about my daughter's artistic genius:
'She's got great skill. D'you think I should send
her to a tutor? He frowned, all artist-serious.
'How old is she now?' 'She's four.'
'I'd beat it out of her,' he said,
'And let's hear of this no more.'
Rightly or wrongly, I encouraged her instead.

She drew me autumn scenes and flowers,
tried to paint *Still Life with Breeze*;
I watched her as she spent long hours
willing her crayons to inspire those trees.
She'd scribble a cartoon that just missed
the essence of the subject, but only just.
'You have to practise,' I'd calmly insist.
She'd look at me gravely. 'You're right, I must.'

Later, I studied the self-portrait in charcoal
she'd done for school, a worthy piece,
but without her life, her éclat, her soul.
Lamely, 'Could you do one of me now please?'
'You're always too still.' This seemed perverse,
but I kind of knew what she must have meant.
And now there was homework, a play to rehearse,
e-mails to write, money to be spent.

'Shall we try a joint effort?' I said at last,
hoping beyond reason it wasn't too late.
'I'm far too busy,' she said, aghast
at the prospect of such an embarrassing fate.

Nowadays we talk, and talk endlessly,
of what we both were trying to achieve;
me, with my maudlin comic poetry,
her with her paintings of what she wished to believe.

The artists. Such a grandiose conceit,
as if showing your mind to the world
was such a big thing. Such self-deceit.
It was always just a father and his little girl.

A COLOUR CHART

When you were seven or so, I'd say,
absorbed by colour anyway,
and your absolute favourite hues
were dusky pinks and pastel blues,
and you would spend undue hours
cataloguing the shades of flowers,
you asked me if I'd redecorate
your bedroom walls when you were eight.

It was a pretty modest request as such.
How much could that cost? I thought, not much.
I invested in a ghastly primrose emulsion.
(Yellow was now your utter compulsion.)
Of course, you hated it not much later
and I had to cover it up with paper
that cost a whole lot more in fact,
though I said nothing, master of tact.

Then, when just a few years had slipped by

you announced you were ready yourself to try

a whole new bedroom colour scheme -

sad, filthy brown and army green.

I thought, my little girl's gone astray,

as you slouched on past me garbed in grey.

You were sampling the colour chart, I see.

But you're in pink today, I note with glee.

MIRRORS

At fifteen or sixteen you'd search beyond my head;
there must be a mirror somewhere, your blue-grey eyes said.
Later, you looked directly at my faded face,
afraid perhaps you were headed to that same place.
Now you gaze at the beauty of your new son's grin
and see yourself not before him, or ahead, but within.

This dimple, that mole, this angling of the eye
a stitch in our knitted fortunes, a sigh
in the rigging of our family tropes.
Our faces reveal not just our but others' hopes;
there are shadows behind the polished glass:
someone from the bright future,
someone from the ghostly past.

And though the mirrors we hold may be flecked
with the mottled doubts we are taught to expect,
as time stains our newness, there's still a chance
we can sing our genes and rejoice in their dance.

THE MIMICS

It started on a train – you doing your 'Rick-ay!'
me grunting my best 'Oh, Biancah!'
the carriage smiling wryly or tutting.
A grown man and his young daughter showing off,
how inappropriate for British Rail.

You sensed a certain disapproval
so promptly switched. 'Oh, Sanjay!'
I knew my 'Gita!' wouldn't impress
so I did my Christopher Walken instead,
I thought this crowd won't recognise
Telly Savalas out of *Kojak* anyway.

And so it went. We'd trade our mimicry
like baseball cards or Happy Families.
I turned to politics, to Major or Tony Blair,
but you couldn't do Thatcher or May –
too shrill for even a proto-Bianca.

And now we do Tigger and Eeyore

and the tiger who came to tea

for my delightful grandson, hoping

on his own journey he will recall all this,

and not tut at his own happy family.

NEW YORKERS

When you were six or seven you opened a bag
belonging to your mother, sniffed inside,
said, 'This bag smells of America'.

Then later, dreaming of that huge world
beyond your mean study bedroom, imagining
all the aromas of all the world's cities,
you told me you'd like to spend
your thirtieth birthday in New York.

I remembered.
And so it came to pass.

We checked in to an hotel on 42nd Street
and looked out at the catwalk of Times Square
with all its idiocies and neon delights.
It was the day before you turned thirty,
A day to appraise what had gone
and what was to, maybe, come.

Five years later you returned the favour
and took me to celebrate my own turning
of the decade; an apartment in Manhattan.
At last I was in my own movie.

We dined at the same restaurant,
though I'd forgotten this subtle place,
saw another Broadway show,
drank crazy priced cocktails at the Top of the Rock.

Who knew one could love like this?
I inhaled my life as if it were new air.

NEW LIFE

The day you told me coyly, 'I'm having a child'
I burst into a babble of all the right phrases
but mainly I remembered your own wild
bursting into life in a little ward. Your face was
gouged by the grief of parturition.
The doctor scored the delivery as a 9
as he softly drew back the partition.
'Nine!' I roared, 'What on earth? She's mine,
and therefore perfect!' He smiled,
as they're trained to do in these places,
and guided me out through a white tiled
hallway to wait for relations to embrace us.

And now I will be someone in that position,
anxious for a scream, a sigh, a sign,
the agony and ecstasy of this strange fission
that leads us only to re-entwine.

WINDSWEPT

Your friends dubbed me 'Windswept'
(maybe kinder than 'Unkempt')
though I tried to take care
of everything but my hair.

You were studious in keeping
me as far away as you could.
'You can pick me up,' you'd declare,
'But make sure to park over there.'

Thirteen is tricky, I've come to understand,
like balancing a biro on an outstretched hand,
or gauging a puddle to leap across.
It also takes much longer than other years.

But the decades for me have caterwauled by,
sweeping hair and hopes up like grime
in their mad stupid dash
to get me finished on time.

I'd like to think you've retained a photo

of the man you tried to conceal

from that girly jury,

as the wind picks up, *voce non sotto.*

PETS

Twice you were robbed of a pet –
a violation for a teenage girl – both times
when we'd returned from a holiday abroad.
The first time when old Carla went to the vet
(she was in pain, the grownups softly said);
the second time when a neighbour admitted
she'd sent our cat Dinah ('I thought it was a stray')
to her daughter who lived far far away.

Neither death nor exile could be countenanced.
You could not forgive, would not speak.
You stayed like that for an agonizing week,
though I called out to you from this new distance.

You've doubled up now – two cats,
two dogs – a spare for each species, I guess,
though you still don't allow me to look after them
and you're deeply suspicious of holidays.

IN THE PADDOCK

Saturday mornings, when it even drizzled in May,
and I was hungover, damp, confused by how early
some people seemed to start their day,
I resented myself for being this surly
but couldn't force the grudging away.

Horse riding lessons, an essential part
of our new life in the country, or nearly,
and you were five years old, good time to start.
But, perched on a morose old beast, clearly
this was not something close to your heart.

The trouble was the actual horse, you said,
too old, too lazy, too bored to move.
All my bones knew all about this, and my head,
but I merely muttered, 'It's bound to improve,'
My heart, like the rain, was grey as lead.

I tried a new tack. 'How does ballet sound?'
(At least I could sit indoors for this)
'Fine.' A pause. 'If it means I can run around.'
We both imagined our different bliss
as we stamped our hooves on the muddy ground.

It still occasionally rains in May
but now it's you that's hungover at eight
and it's me that wants to run and play,
and I wonder, as I lean against a garden gate,
where are all the wild horses that got away.

BOYFRIENDS

A father is always afraid
for his daughter.
This is true as the sun,
as certain as taxes.
I was no exception.

I met each new suitor
(though they wouldn't have
called themselves that)
with a wincing eye
and a firm handshake.

One was polite but too wan;
another too arrogant;
a third more attentive
to his trainers and jeans
than your welfare, I felt.

They trailed in and out
not knowing they were
ill prepared interviewees.
I wondered whether
you would end up alone.

And now I'm debating
the fortunes of our team,
the latest debacle,
the chance of good weather
with the man who's my son-in-law.

I should have quieted my fears,
relied on your judgement, known
you would know who and when.
He has daughters too
and, I'm sure, fears of his own.

MAKING

You an artist, a designer,
alert to shape and form
and pattern and colour;
me a writer of sorts,
a worrier of tangling words,
a wrangler of meaning.

You would have thought us
the ideal combo.
And we tried.
We sat, as if at a partner's desk,
and struggled to make a book
together.

What we fashioned at last
was worthy, but
'not for the market'
our agent affirmed.
She was younger even than you.
'Try blogging,' she said.

What we made in the end

was more enduring than that.

We made laughter

as we coloured in words

and crafted a new kind

of self-portraiture.

SIBLINGS

You fought with your brothers
as if they were barbarians
at the gate of your
decent sensibilities.

One would steal a ruler,
another use a scrunchy
for a catapult.
Always the rows over food,
as if there'd never be more.

I'd try to umpire it all,
a finger raised,
as if that would do.
And still the uncivil wars
would roll on, the cries
of dismay like a mother
who's lost her cubs.

Nothing ever was fair.
No one understood.
Except we all did,
had suffered like you
in our own conscription.

You get on famously now,
and recall all your battles
like generals in some parlour
of a rarified club.
Sometimes, I like to imagine,
I'm mentioned in dispatches.

WHEN YOU CHANGED

You were spindly twelve;
I was sturdy forty five and
already collapsing to
a sack of sad stuff on a settee,
pummelled useless by work.

You came bouncing into the room
dressed in your mother's clothes,
lipsticked and made up
model-fancy, your eyes wide aglow
with the certainty of approval.

I was horrified.
Your yards-wide grin slowed down
as you approached the settee,
nervous as a ruminant
at a waterhole.

'I'm still your little girl,' you said.

(Sometimes a father needs comforting).

'I was just trying on some things.

I'll go and change back.'

'No you won't', I nearly said.

MAN AND WOMAN

JUNE 1st 2016

It's not as if I hadn't been through it before –

the registrar's mellifluous assurances,

the blur of relatives in wedding-best,

a new gold ring burning a hole in my hand –

but this was different. An amazing foreign land.

We hadn't chosen music – something jolly, something serious

but fifty yards away I could almost hear

the choir of gulls and the sea's dull timpani.

The registry is next to Swansea beach.

And I heard mermaids singing each to each.

I was finally together. Made whole, and now in public so.

I love you Rachel. You are my North by North.

As for me, I'd "scrubbed up well" they said,

but you looked so frightened-happy that fine day.

We mumbled things you're told to say and sailed away.

And danced in Noah's wine bar, our little Ark,
to Simon and Garfunkel's Bridge Street song.
We'd come to watch all sorts of flowers growing
and family and friends looked on in quiet awe.
One said, "He'd only shown disappointment before."

THE BEAR, COWBRIDGE

10 November 2006

It's winter and I'm here once more at The Bear,
gazing at careworn wood and stone.
I'm drinking latté, not Guinness or beer,
and I'm tranquil enough at being alone,
though I wish it was summer and you were here.

The years pass by like motorway signs
- high-sided urgencies hide them from sight –
and it's good to pause for this moment in time
to think about us, our winter nights,
but I wish it was summer and you were mine.

We've been alive in pubs and free
in Cheltenham, Chepstow, Worcester, Hay,
racing down Cointreau, rum, G & T,
but this is a moribund sort of day,
and I wish it was Summer and you were with me.

It can't be all Budapest Rome and Paris:
at times we smile and jointly know
that it's good to stretch out on our settee terrace.
I'm glad of Winter's dark and snow,
but I wish it was summer and we were in Arras.

I'll be home tonight for the weekend's haze,
to our own good wood, our time together,
our football, our peace, our laughing ways,
and I'll love it all madly now and forever,
for it's always Summer these brilliant days.

ACTUALLY

You ask me what I love, apart from you.
Now, there comes it flapping
at my swollen heart. Here,
and no step further in this sand.

I love, of course, the thrill
of winning, and if not me,
the team I decided would be mine,
whoever plays for them.

I love, like breathing,
my children's oval smiles,
their human curiosity at being alive,
their utter sense of right.

I love, but hate, each cigarette,
each half-baked, half-born poem,
each dusk that breaks the bloom
and blankness of each day.

I quite like trees, their ambiguity,
and water, with its swirling permanence,
and houses, though they swear
and lie they'll never leave.

But all these things are loaned to me;
I love them, though they will not last.
I'd let the lot of them all go
for you, your smile, your kiss, your sigh.

You ask me what I love apart from you.
There's only you.
You are what makes me live and love.
Apart from you, there's nothing.

FALLING

We'd meet in pubs, those lunchtime days,

me sneaking off work

you perhaps just having got up.

The pub with the clock with no hands,

the one with the garden with the tree

where we imagined sausages grew,

the one in the maze of streets

where vagabond kids sprouted.

They'd be kicking a ball, and each other.

We'd talk or play darts,

clack balls around baize

or re-watch the movie

that was always on in the corner of the bar.

It was the days when people smoked,

so we did, and with gusto.

It was always sunny outside,

it seems to me now,

though rain must have fallen

silently, with furtive feet,

like the love which crept up on us

and said 'Boo!'

Thank god we were not afraid.

I was always falling you see,

hoping you'd not be afraid to catch me.

BUILDING PLANS

If I could build for you a perfect home
I'd build it out of driftwood and wet sand.
I'd build it where the subtle sand crabs roam
and shuffling water meets our ragged land.

I'd build like Gaudi, no straight line or plane;
perhaps an igloo teardrop edifice,
where sunlight settles and where gulls complain
and where there is no dizzying precipice.

This place between what's solid and what flows
is where our hope resides and whence it springs;
where we consider what we think we know,
that everything is made of other things,

Let's decorate our dreams with shells today
as we progress along the crescent bay.

LOST AND FOUND

Shiftless on a sudden Spring morning
I looked out at the ragged borders,
the sneaking weeds,
considered the shed,
with its musty hoes
and hoses and trowels:

Ah, the fetid promise,
hmmm, the dark dread,
then decided to tidy up instead.

I rummaged the cupboards and drawers -
so many dried up pens
and unsent cards,
so many batteries and wires,
those grey bits of plastic
from god knows where –
till I laid my hand on this,
a slim red leather address book.

Here, the past stepped forward,

bowed awkwardly

at the unexpected curtain call.

So many names –

a plumber, a long retired dentist,

a carpet fitter called Wally,

a builder aptly called Jerry.

Then the people with bigger parts -

some former friends I'd forgotten,

an uncle and some cousins

their numbers crossed out

as they moved or divorced

or just didn't answer.

And then you,

no surname, just you,

with the telephone number

that we brought to this house.

How can you be there, amongst

the dead and the neglected,

the desiccated and the discarded,

and yet you're here,

so beautiful, so laughing,

where my life blooms?

PERFECT DAY

It's a perfect day

when

> you overhear laughter
>
> careering out of an open window

when

> you wake before you need to
>
> and it pleases you

when

> the rain and the sun agree
>
> to take a stroll together across the sky

when

> the pastry falls apart
>
> in your astonished mouth

when

> the violin, in soaring,
>
> makes a man's eyes fill

when

> you find those keys, that ten pound note,
> those words to say what you mean

It's a perfect day

when

> the cherry tree bursts into white
> or the letter arrives and you're clear

when

> your ache subsides
> as I stroke your back

when

> you smile at me
> for no other reason than love

when

> your eyes dance delight
> at some unbidden courtesy

Then, lover, then

GOOD MORNING, DREAMER

On rare occasions I wake before you, gaze
at the tousle of hair, the bedclothes cast aside,
one arm splayed out, the other by your side
as if you were practicing your own chalk outline,
and I touch your warmth, smile at my own relief.
Sometimes I even speak, dare to disturb,
but softly, in case you're dreaming of me,
or something good, a place you go to run free.

I'll slide out of bed like a cat round a corner
and let you rest here alive but moveless,
your mind floating in the lovely wind
of whatever dream it is, even if it's not me.

QUIET TIMES AT THE DINNER TABLE

When I see that first muscle crease
of a grimace
as I lay down the plate
with a ta da!
I know that boeuf bourgignon
is a misjudgement.

Somewhere in the past
someone's Bisto'd it to death,
and spoiled this dish for us.

You're too polite to say
and you praise instead
the perfectly sautéed potatoes,
the bright greenness of the peas;
whatever you can to please.

Tomorrow I'll do sea bass or trout,
though it's not the actual food, I know.
It's the sharing, that refrain

in our orchestra of eating.

The quiet nod

at another refueling of our love.

THE ASHES

In the backroom of a bar in Prague,
the floor covering ochre linoleum,
the bench seating red Rexene,
two men are craning their still heads
upwards and behind at a wall mounted TV.
It's The Ashes and a fierce young Brett Lee.
We are watching the drama too,
hands interlocked, Pilsner for the moment
untouched, too bitter, irrelevant.

We're the only people in the bar –
life outside thrums carelessly by –
and the over is lasting forever
as the last two Aussies try to ease
their way to shocking victory.
Then Kasprowicz gloves the ball behind
and Flintoff crouches to comfort Lee.
A moment of manly humility.
You captured it on your phone for posterity.

Then three years later in another back room,

this time in a village near Upper Cwm Twrch,

we saw the same two men, still silent and still.

Then one spoke: 'You're the girl who took that photo

of the TV in Prague, in that bar.'

Our hands were still interlocked

as they will always be. 'That's right,'

you said, 'The Ashes, 2005'

The sweet lingering taste of victory.

FISH FOR THOUGHT

The size of those sardines – astonishing –
who could ever have known
that outside a tin they could grow
to be ingots of silver like these?

Or that sea bass in Chepstow? It dripped off the
edges of your plate like a Dali painting.
And prawns, massive curlicues of meat,
tanned gold in garlic and olive oil.

A dorada in Greece, a swordfish in Sicily.
Your opal eyes glowed, opened like a cat's
at these fishy delights
those balmy huge-mooned tender nights.

I love sitting opposite you,
watching you relish what is good,
as I pick through the detritus
of my corned beef hash.

A CHILDISH FANCY

We brought kids to our marriage,
kids from before.
But we both wanted more.

I wanted a new son to win trophies,
a new daughter to win hearts
(or the other way round);
to somehow repeat myself,
only better, a version
of all that could be
if life was not so cobbled.

You wanted a baby,
not a miniature of yourself,
but a tiny face to adore your eyes;
a little limbed thing, happy to be.
And happy to be hugged
within an inch of its life.

Such progeny would have realised

that its perilous voyage

into the gaping world

was no accident,

no mere urge made flesh,

but the sum of something,

and the sum of something good.

And loved us for this, but then perhaps

grown to deplore us

for pushing it forward

and holding it back

in the seesaw of loving and hoping.

THE DENDROPHILES

The desire to grow – radishes, lettuce,

anything really, daffodils,

pungent mint, tiny carrots,

foul smelling bay leaves,

more courgettes than we'd ever need.

We ripped up the concrete

swept up the gravel

laid a new lawn,

hunted down dandelions,

yearned for snowdrops.

Then we bought three trees –

cherry , apple and pear –

(though the apple turned out

to be another pear) and lined

them up by our neighbour's wall.

The dendrophile instinct surged in us,

the sweep of a branch, the shade,

 the swell of the fruit.

the petal delicateness,

the bulk of the bole.

I love our trees. I watch their sway

from a kitchen window,

admire their stubborn desire to live

whatever the elements throw at them.

I should learn from their strength, their ease.

CHANGING THE WORLD

Though adults, and some,
we giggled like children
over midnight snacks
and Cointreau
and Captain Morgan
and wine from the local shop.

We just had to talk
though work tomorrow
whistled shrilly
and waved its cards at us.
We wanted to change the world.

Two lovers discussing
religion and politics,
witchcraft and poetry,
past partners, lost relatives,
our childhood confectionery choices,
music and movies and sport.

We talked as if on a journey,
an engine hurtling us elsewhere
though we were always here.
We forgot to go to bed
in the fusion of words.

In a way,
we realised much later,
we were changing the world,
and, I'm sure, for the better.

PARTY PEOPLE

That December party in our new house:
you wearing one glove
as you practised your putting
with your new golf clubs
on our smooth new carpet,
for we had no furniture.

In the kitchen a workmate
and one of our children
dueting a Simon and Garfunkel
on my old guitar
with no one listening.

In another room
people looking at pictures,
reading titles of books,
admiring our gifts to each other.

I mixed mad cocktails

for the newly elected members

of our new broad church:

a couple of mutual friends

but the rest newly met and melded.

It was noise and laughing

with no points of order.

We had a manifesto though.

Unwritten, unpublished

but solid as these old house walls.

Our love will last a thousand years.

THE MINIATURISTS

Gripped silly by a sudden notion
I raced to the off licence.
Then, clutching a clinking carrier bag,
I proudly presented tonight's gift:
two dozen miniatures.

A violent emerald crème de menthe,
two Cointreaus (Cointreaux?),
a Bailey's, a crème de cacao,
Drambuie, Southern Comforts (3),
Amaretto, Kahlua, Advocaat,
Tia Maria, crème de cassis,
and aptly, Parfait d'Amour.

You spurned the too sweet Grand Marnier,
but tolerated limoncello.
Sambuca, Disaronno, Eblana,
Green Chartreuse, a tad sickly.
Jägermeister, spoiled for you
by bombing juveniles,

a sip of anisette, a whiff of pastis,
(these two taste the same, you said)

We chicaned through the hair-raising
debauchery of it all,
the Reeves palette of crazy booze
in all those variegated hues,
till it was time to make love again,
though of course we'd been making it
all the drunk while.

UP TO ELEVEN

We come from different generations:
mine defined by The Who,
yours by the New Romantics
(to sixties me The Romantics were
either Blake and Wordsworth
or Ruby's backing singers).*

But we found a thumping middle ground
In Chas and Dave rabbiting to an old Joanna,
and Afroman's 'Cos I got high'.
(Our own highs after all
were endless laughter and talking).

You smiled to jolly Cliff Richard,
I sighed at doleful Bob Dylan,
but we sat down together and gazed
out over Otis's 'Dock of the Bay'.
(We'd both left our homes in Georgia
but everything was coming our way).

We'd stay up through acres of night,

though our vinyl childhoods

were stolen or gone,

and we'd dance or just sing super loud

to Madness's mad 'Our House'.

These mellow days we're up to eleven,

but not like Spinal Tap;

more like Johnny Mathis or Matt Monroe,

or in your case, perhaps, Adele.

*Ruby and the Romantics 'Our Day Will Come', Kapp
Records, 1962

WHERE DO WE GO NEXT?

You didn't like downtown Manhattan,
too loud, too brash, too racy, too far,
I thought Tunisia a hot mistake,
and I didn't enjoy that journey to the Loire.

We weren't much fussed on Adelaide;
Crete was too quiet, too flat, too dull;
Gran Canaria was a soporific bore,
and neither of us really liked Portugal.

We missed our flight in Sydney that time;
we argued in Rome in the Eton Hotel;
Switzerland in summer was wrong
and the hills in Murcia were sheer hell.

But I'll never forget the waiter in Tallinn,
his horror at our menu choices,
nor the Hermitage in St Petersburg
and that sudden choir of Russian voices.

And London, ah London, Stow-on-the-Wold,
Amsterdam, Prague and Budapest,
the days in the anonymous Jeanne D'Arc
and even those evenings in Haverfordwest.

And Iceland's swirling electric skies,
geysers and lava and pure pure water;
that old chef pointing to our waitress
and saying with trembling pride, 'mi dochter!'

But above all in the swelter of mid July
cool Alsace lager in an Arras square,
a Moroccan meal near The Moulin Rouge;
oh how I yearn to be with you there.

I dream of our journeys to other lands.
Not to be elsewhere, I'm in love with here,
but simply just being alone with you.
So, my darling, where to go next year?

MAN

THE TWO OF US

I, that entity I half know, half don't,
am more than that, that one bare thing.
I'm two at least, the will, the won't,
the parts that fight to cleave and cling.

A bifurcated brain and heart
that find it hard to comprehend
divided loyalties, when we're
both shuffling to one united end.

An outer shell that laughs in derision
at other's follies and pecadilloes;
an inner softer muscle with no vision,
in thrall to worries, fears and woes.

One self rushed off to seek out fame,
or something of that nebulous sort;
the other hid its head in shame
at such unconscionable sport.

The two of us, the I, the me,
we should have resolved within the womb
the lifelong struggle, the mystery
of how to fit into the tomb.

But on we go on our different roads
staggering or strutting, according to taste,
struggling to adjust our aching loads,
trying to salvage good from the waste.

My shadow throws some spiteful shade
at all the juvenile impertinence
and all the promises we made
when we danced as youngsters together once.

But we'll waltz again one blazing day,
gripping each other by the fist;
the shy, introverted, sad gourmet,
the garrulous, egregious egotist.

ENCOMIUM

You shouldn't write your own encomium,
it smacks of hubris, dishonest grandeur,
like the bishop who ordered his own fine tomb
(though perhaps in language somewhat blander).

My own periphrastic, prolix tone
should tell me before I tap a key
that words are only words alone
and not honest autobiography.

I'll just say this: I really tried
to see myself, and say myself too,
to get at what was locked inside,
until I saw it was simply you.

What last words uttered one solemn day
about a man whose hundred was hit
should be muttered and allowed to float away,
and let that be the end of it.

THE IMPOSTER

I write so that I may perhaps discover
what I thought I was thinking yesterday:
the curve or sumptuous sweep of my lover,
haeccitas, eros, or even *agape?*

Or mere mundanity, the dull slow thud
of lowly life lived dully day to day;
the impudent corpuscles in the blood
striking for better conditions or more pay?

Thus the imposter, the shoulder monkey,
that jealous gremlin whispering in my ear.
We argue daily, me pleading like a junkie:
'Just one more fix, then you can disappear.'

The new day bursts, I write so I can free
our surly selves from this dichotomy.

(UN)BELIEVER

I read the King James Bible
tatty cardboard cover to cover.
I tried a paperback Quran but struggled.
At fifteen I hadn't even heard
of Baghavad Gita
or Guru Granth Sahib,
not that Ralph's,
the secondhand bookshop
I frequented like a virus,
would have stocked such things.

There were bits that vaguely intrigued
but mainly it was the usual parables
and the all too tedious homilies.
So I tried a bit of Wordsworth,
till daffodils and small celandines
were coming out of my ears,
but nature didn't strike me as my goddess.

How to believe?

I tried out myself,

like the self-help books said,

but I was not trustworthy,

a soft serpent in my own garden.

One side of me wanted to pray,

to somehow account for the mysteries;

the other said doubt is okay;

there is only the one certainty.